Apocalypse Now?

Seeing Beyond The Veil

Ruth L. Miller, Ph.D.

Apocalypse Now?

Seeing Beyond
The Veil

Ruth L. Miller, Ph.D.

Portal
Center
Press

Apocalypse Now? Seeing Beyond the Veil
© 2020 Ruth L. Miller, Ph.D.

Portal Center Press
www.portalcenterpress.com

cover photo:"Fire Puja at Wake & Kinlan's" by Barbara Grundeman

ISBN: 978-1-936902-38-5

ebook edition isbn: 978-1-936902-37-8

Printed in the USA

Appreciation

Many thanks to all those people who have supported my work and to those many more who are supporting this amazing process we're going through – this "lifting of the veil" into a world that's been hidden from our view.

Contents

Introduction

Contrary to our usual understanding, the term "Apocalypse" does not mean a one-time, disastrous event in which the current world is destroyed and a new kind of world replaces it. Far from it. In fact, the word is the Greek term for the process by which a bridegroom lifts the veil of his never-seen-before bride and observes for the first time the woman who, through the sacred ritual of marriage, will be his companion, helper, and teacher for the rest of his life.

Apocalypse, then, is a process. It's the process of discovery, a process of wishes and dreams becoming experiential reality, a process by which two youths – bride and groom – begin to become adults.

Each of us goes through such a process several times in our lives. We move along, guided by dreams and wishes and hope, then the experience becomes real to our physical senses and we begin a new stage in our life's journey. Each time we create something or achieve a dreamed-of goal or enter a new phase in our life or career, we have an apocalyptic experience.

Historians applied the term to the New Testament book, The Revelation of John, because it was one of hundreds of apocalyptic writings being written after Rome destroyed Jerusalem and dispersed the Judaic people through the empire.

These letters and books were filled with fear and angst about what was happening, but they also offered hope for a new and different kind of life. Many of them were prophetic in the classic sense of the term: they voiced the words and thoughts of God. As such, they revealed, and offered, a deeper understanding and connection with the divine in a time of chaos, fear, and misery.

The word revelation is also about seeing what wasn't seen before, experiencing a deeper understanding, comprehending what had been incomprehensible, and, in religious terms, experiencing divinely revealed truths.

The world today, in the year 2020, is once more filled with fears, distress, and longings - and also apocalypses and revelations. Many of them affect individuals and communities; others affect the whole world. With global media and the fact that anyone with a camera and the internet can tell the whole world what they are seeing, thousands of people can share whatever anyone has experienced in a matter of seconds. So YouTube, Facebook, and other social media are bombarded with ever new, more powerful, descriptions of dreams and visions that explain what's happening and what we must prepare for.

This little book explores the nature of our current apocalypse and its implications, and offers some ways we can all "lift the veil."

An Ongoing Process

Looking back may give us some idea of the pattern that is unfolding, and provide clearer insights about what's happening in the present and the future. So that's where we'll start.

The last century could be said to be an ongoing series of apocalypses for people in European and American culture, as each decade brought new insights and deeper understandings, amid frequent appearances that the world was coming to an end. In fact, it could be said that each generation has experienced their own apocalyptic event.

A Half-century of Massive Change

THE 1910S

By the second decade of the 20th century each of those conceptual breakthroughs was established within their respective communities of thought and experience. Then a whole new set of ideas began to percolate, based in part on the the 1860s' works of Karl Marx and Frederic Engels. The Russian revolution launched a global awareness of the possibility, which, some say, is what sparked the action that led to the first World War, involving virtually all of Europe and North America, as much of the Middle East and Japan. The same period saw the emergence of airplanes as a way to get things done – both mil-

3

itarily and commercially. That war ended and was immediately followed by a viral epidemic that wiped out huge populations of Europe and the US and led to the formation of a new kind of healthcare system, based on a new assumption: that the community as a whole was responsible for the well-being of its members.

THE 1920S

The "Roaring 20s" are famous, possibly, because of humanity's determination to "roar back" after the decimation of the first World War and the viral infection that followed, but mostly because the spirit of revolution was alive in the hearts and minds of young people everywhere, and they challenged the status quo in every way they could. They tried new ways of relating, of dressing, of eating and drinking, and expanded their ideas of what was acceptable entertainment to include influences from other cultures, including the jazz of African-Americans. This was also the decade of the missionary: young people from Europe and America moved to what they were told were spiritually and physically impoverished regions of the world to "save souls and heal bodies." Many of them spent the rest of their lives living in these new worlds and sharing them with people "back home." Others spent a few years overseas and then returned home to teach and work, bringing new levels of understanding about the world "out there" with them.

THE 1930S

The collapse of the New York Stock Exchange in 1929 defined the shape of life in the 1930s around the world. People who had enjoyed great wealth were suddenly impoverished. People who had come to depend on selling their products to those wealthy people were suddenly impoverished. Governments that had come to depend on taxes from those others were suddenly impoverished. The system of mutual growth no longer functioned and no one had a clue what to do. Missions and Settlement Houses were set up in urban neighborhoods to help folks deal with poverty and, hopefully, move on from it, but that didn't help the failing farmer or factory worker.

This was the Great Depression, and it inspired a new idea: the idea that government could and should take a role in guaranteeing everyone's wellbeing. In the US, Franklin Roosevelt offered a way for that to happen, uplifting peoples' hearts with the theme song "Happy Days Are Here Again." Governments applied an old war tactic to what was a seemingly impossible situation: they began to spend money they didn't have to hire lots of people to do great projects for the good of the people. In the US those WPA projects in national parks and forests still remain as monuments to that era. Slowly, worldwide, people began to emerge from the depths of an economic crisis that no one believed could have happened and nearly everyone except small, self-sustaining communities, suffered from.

THE 1940s

The close of the '30s and the end of the Depression was the beginning of yet another great war. World War II lasted from 1939 to 1945, involved even more nations than WWI, and was as much a war of ideas and technologies as of battlefield tactics. New kinds of weapons systems, with new kinds of vessels – on land, in the sea, and in the air – were constantly being introduced throughout the war years. A whole new approach to developing and managing projects emerged in the process, and the "Think Tank," merging science and engineering to address complex problems, was born.

Across the US and Europe, men and women were introduced to other nations and ways of living, as they were moved around in the military, and for jobs to support the military. These experiences meant that the second half of the 1940s was a time of redefining who we were and how we wanted life to be – individually and collectively. The production capacity created to meet the demands of the war was turned to meeting the needs of thousands of new citizen-consumers as new families were formed, often thousands of miles away from the homes they grew up in and therefore needing new homes and equipment to manage them.

A huge number of children, becoming known as the "Baby-boom" generation, was born in brand new hospitals and grew up in brand new housing developments in the suburbs of large cities that were centers of industry, commerce, and culture. Franklin Roosevelt's government, continuing their Depression-era practices, paid returning soldiers and sailors to buy homes and get a college education – making what had been limited to about 10% of the population available to virtually everyone. In Europe and Japan, cities that had been utterly destroyed by the new technologies were being rebuilt with US funds and equipment, and there, too, children grew up in new homes with few if any ties to older generations and ways of thinking.

THE 1950S

So the 1950s was, in many ways, a new way of living – unlike anything in humanity's history. The difference between the world of the 1950s and the world of the 1900s was far greater than the world of the 1900s had been from the world of the 1600s. People who lived through the first half of the 20th century went from farms and small shops on dirt and wooden roads, with a few steamships, trains, and factories, to jet planes and cars and paved streets and skyscrapers and huge industrial complexes, from large extended families living close together – often in the same house – to nuclear and single-parent families, isolated in suburbs and apartments, and using telephones to stay connected.

And that very term "nuclear" was totally new: the weapons developers of WWII had built on the work of the first part of the century to unleash the power of the atom in the world, making the words "atomic" and "nuclear" household terms –

and the fear of an atomic holocaust a household concern. Schoolchildren were taught how to protect themselves from an atomic attack in the same way they had been taught to protect themselves in Europe during the bombings of the war, and the military spent huge amounts of money and resources to protect the US and Europe from such an attack.

Then, in the mid-1950s the post-war boom began to slow down, but the production capacity was still in place, and people still remembered and feared the agony of the Depression. So companies hired experts to figure out how to convince people they needed to buy more things in order to keep the factories working – and the profits coming into the shareholders' pockets. Thus was created "Madison Avenue" marketing. Their advertisements were applied to everything: from what we read to what we ate to what we heard on the radio – and it worked! Without the support of extended families and lacking a deep connection with "home," isolated housewives were vulnerable to the marketing ploys of the "Ad men" and succumbed. Particularly in the US, the acquisition of things replaced the building of relationships as a primary source of fulfillment. Only a few thoughtful people saw what was happening and expressed concern.

The Turning Point of the 1960s

Now there was the largest ever generation of children who had grown up isolated from their extended families, in a world where anything they might want or need was available, amid a constant stream of advertising telling them what more they might want or need, and the expectation that, if the world did not end by war first, they, too, would go to college and get an even better life than the one their parents had lived while raising them. They came into adolescence in the 1960s. and, as all adolescents do, began the process of deciding who they were, of individuating from their parents. Only their parents weren't just the people who gave birth to them, it was the whole world: the schools, the churches, the government, and the media that surrounded them.

How does one individuate when the whole world has become one's parent – and there is no rite of passage to ease one into adulthood? That was the unconscious driver that led to what became known as the "Hippy" movement, with its characteristics of "sex, drugs, and rock'n'roll," and demands for "no more war." Their parents had short or carefully coifed hair? Well then, we'll have long, messy hair. They wore bras and girdles or 3-piece suits, with shiny leather pumps? Then we'll wear long, loose, flowing dresses and shirts, with denim pants and sandals. They wanted to listen to melodious music with an easy rhythm? Then we'll choose raucus tones and off beats for our music. They worked 9-5 to earn the money to get things? Then we'll refuse to take a job and find other ways to get what we want and need. They lived quiet lives of desperation in isolated houses in the suburbs?

Then we'll move a whole bunch of like-minded people into a house in the city and love on each other. They were law-abiding citizens, accepting what the government told them? Then we'll protest and refuse to do what we're told – which led to new legislation around civil rights, new approaches in the education system, and new limits on employers. Then the US put a man on the moon. And the world changed once more.

Another thing that was happening in the 1960s got a lot less attention in the media, but will probably have even longer-term effects on the world. People were noticing that the natural world was suffering from the things humanity was doing and air- and water-protection acts were passed in the US and some other countries. People were also developing tools for understanding how something that appeared to be a simple act could have widespread consequences. The fields of ecology and cybernetics emerged in the 1950s, took root in the 1960s, and evolved into environmental studies and systems thinking in the 1970s. The books *Silent Spring* and *Tragedy of the Commons*, combined with the annual *Whole Earth Catalog*, made an impact on people's thinking and began to affect their actions in ways that will continue to be felt for many more decades.

THE 1970S

The 1970s saw a break-up into splinters of what had seemed, for many people, to be a homogenous worldview and way of life back in the

1940s and '50s. This apparent homogeneity is what the people who call themselves "Conservatives" and whom Paul Ray calls "Traditionals" in his book *Cultural Creatives*, are longing to return to. But by the '70s it was apparent to most that such a return was not likely – and that homogeneity may never even have existed.

Many of the adolescents of the 1960s found themselves raising children or wanting to make a difference in the world, so they went back to school and became "Young Urban Professionals" or "Yuppies". Continuing the pattern set in their childhoods, they created isolated, nuclear or single-parent families who acquired more and more things while they sought fulfillment in their work.

Their children, the "X" generation, got very mixed messages about what was right and what was wrong: much of their education coming from the television, ranging from the happy intercultural messages of *Sesame Street* to the intensity of cop-and-robber programming, with advertisements everywhere. Their schools were still overcrowded and understaffed and were now getting conflicting directions on what to teach and how. Their parents were also conflicted, wishing the dreams of the Hippy days had been fulfilled while they worked 9-5 (or much longer) 5-6 days a week to provide for their families, while the definition of "provide for" was expanding every year – including new technologies and hardware, more education, and more vehicles per person.

In the meantime, the industrial production facilities built during and after WWII were wearing out, and companies began looking for lower-cost alternatives. At the same time a very strange thing happened: US states began to make it easy for anyone to incorporate a business, separating the owners from any effects their products or production methods might have on the consumers – and shifting the focus of business from a few people producing high quality products and maintaining good relationships with customers to a faceless entity with a legal requirement to maximize dividends for the shareholders.

With all this, the definition of "middle class" began to shift, which had much greater political and economic impacts than could be foreseen at the time.

The Transformative Technology of the '80s

Although it began in the 1970s, it wasn't until the 1980s that the media – and therefore the general public – realized that a whole new world was being transformed by computer engineers in what was soon dubbed "Silicon Valley". The strip of land between Stanford University and the IBM design facility is less than 50 miles along the San Andreas fault, south of San Francisco. Mostly farmland in the 1960s, by the '80s it was covered with suburban housing and industrial parks. Think tanks of every sort had been functioning in the area since WWII, and the old zeppelin hangers at Moffett field on the Bay had been home to NASA and Lockheed engineers since the early 1970s.

At that time computers, invented during WWII, were large, complex machines requiring lots of money, their own space, and highly trained, intelligent people to operate them. Many companies were involved in that industry, but IBM was the leader in designing, installing, and maintaining the monsters. Then, in a couple of garages in Silicon Valley, two different teams of people came up with two very different approaches: one was the Apple line, put together by students and rebels; the other was the Hewlett-Packard line, put together by corporate engineers. They each found a way to transform the electronic monster into something people could relate to, and even carry!

Innovations by other companies and individuals in the region led to greater refinements and introduced the new, small computers into the classroom as teaching aids, but it was the promotion of the spreadsheet, Visicalc, in 1978, that brought the personal computer into the rest of the world. With this piece of software, for the first time in corporate history, a manager could sit down and figure out in a matter of minutes what had always taken their accounting or data-processing department days or weeks to solve: what would happen if... What would it cost me to raise a salary? What would reducing the price on this mean? What if I could combine these processes...? It was magic! Now, all at once, a CEO or mid-level manager or someone starting a new business had the capacity to figure out what the options really were.

In a few years this capacity made it possible for a whole new generation of entrepreneurs to emerge, not requiring nearly as much funding as before, leading to an entirely new possibility of experiencing satisfaction in one's work. It also meant that people who didn't have computers were now at a disadvantage, and those who had been doing the work that computers now did were losing their jobs, which led to another wave of corporate layoffs – so many learned how to make the computer their helper instead of their replacement, using the new equipment and software, leading to another wave of development.

These constant waves of technological development made it impossible for highly structured institutions – private or public – to survive. They simply didn't have the flexibility to adapt and continue. And one of those was the government that was trying to hold together the Union of Soviet Socialist Republics. Instantaneous exchanges of information around the world could not be stopped and so the USSR, which had been seen as the probable source of attack on Europe and the US for three decades, began to crumble – the Berlin Wall being taken over by young people was the first evidence of that visible in the US.

They also led many individuals to question the tried-and-true methods of working and living they'd been taught – and to wonder if there could be a better way. They began to study psychology, religion, and philosophy looking for answers, and to share the answers they found, thus launching another new wave: the Self-help movement, which offered an optimistic view of possibilities and the potential to get past current issues.

THE 1990S

As a result the 1990s opened with an explosion of enthusiasm around the world – the Apocalypse of Armageddon was no longer imminent! A new wave of capitalism spread across Eastern Europe and Asia. The countries of Europe formed an economic union and let go of old requirements for passports and different forms of money for travelers between their nations. Computers and computer-based companies drove economies and education. Innovation was the name of the game. Even in the stodgiest of industries, like banking, this attitude led to a new set of products being offered to maximize profits (because, remember, a corporation is legally required to maximize dividends to its shareholders, and most US companies were corporations by then).

Computers were everywhere in business and education in the '90s, but much less in peoples' personal lives. It wasn't until a little experiment in computer networking was expanded across the US that computers truly became "personal." During the 1970s the military had created a computer network that allowed them to control operations from a distance. Called ARPANET

(Advanced Research Projects Access Network), it allowed computers – and soon, using teletype machines, their operators – to communicate from one installation to another. In the late 1970s the US government invited a few universities to join this network and immediately, collaborative research was expanded significantly. So, using phone lines at first, and then, with the introduction of satellite-based, high-speed cable-tv networks, it became possible for anyone, anywhere, to share information via their computers in a matter of seconds. University researchers could exchange results instantly. Business and government offices could share, not only oral message by telephone, but written messages by what became known as "electronic mail" or email. And, as the bandwidth expanded and the computers had more memory, pictures could be shared.

As the processors were made smaller and faster, more and more data could be shared across the cable lines. Companies and agencies that had been operating as islands were now operating as one whole entity. The media took a while to catch up, but when they did, it meant that anyone, anywhere, could know what was going on wherever in the country – and the world. People watched television programs from hundreds of countries. They saw images of whatever they were interested in, wherever it was located.

There was so much data, in fact, that people were in overload. They didn't know how to find what they were looking for anymore – there were thousands of needles in haystacks, and no way to know how to start. It's been suggested that some of the economic ups and downs of the 1990s were simply a function of not being able to track all the information that was coming in. So data management and representation began to emerge as a new field, and Search Engines were the next development. Computers had made file clerks obsolete, but data managers could help people track all that information inside the little boxes on their desk and help them find it when they needed it.

Still, in the background, more and more people were seeing that our industries and transportation – even our farms and households – were causing more damage to the air, water, and soil, and that patterns in the ocean and the atmosphere were starting to change. The United Nations held an international conference on the environment in Brazil in 1992, leading to a major agreement among nations to begin to address the problems. One of the outcomes of that meeting was that indigenous peoples from around the world got together and, in spite of having very different languages and customs, were able to make a combined statement to the governments whose actions affected their lands and ways of life. Through the decade non-governmental organizations were formed, each with a specific focus on shifting from exploiting and destroying natural resources to recovering and regenerating them.

A New Century Begins

As the year 2000 approached, governments, businesses, and many individuals were totally dependent on their computer networks for storing and exchanging information, and someone realized that all those forms, all those tables, and all those calendars were based on dates starting with 19... What would happen when the date started with 20...? Wouldn't it mess up the computers? And wouldn't that cause the collapse of all the institutions that relied on them? This Y2K phenomenon turned into a massive scare, and the word Apocalypse once more entered peoples' conversations in the US, as well as Europe, India, and other countries who had bought into the computer revolution. For some observers it was as if the fear of a nuclear-war based Armageddon was replaced with a fear of electronic meltdown. And, of course, hundreds of computer experts were put to work to "fix" it and January 1, 2000 did not see the much-feared (and perhaps hoped for?) collapse of the economies or the governments of the industrialized nations.

What it saw, instead, was a new idea of what the world is. Thousands of people celebrated the New Year together, as it moved around the planet from time zone to time zone, recognizing that this is one planet with one people.

Then the unthinkable happened: a few young men from Saudi Arabia hijacked some jet airliners and flew them into very carefully chosen targets: the World Trade Center (home offices of several leading companies in international finance) in New York City, a part of the Pentagon (home offices of the US military) that was under construction, and another target that was missed because some young American men sacrificed themselves to crash the plane and prevent it from accomplishing its mission. It was the 11th of September, 2001. The world was stunned. Was this the start of Armaggedon? Had the Apocalyptic events of Revelation begun? Air traffic was grounded, everywhere around the US for 3 days – during which skies that had been hazy with contrails became clear and only the faintly disturbing sound of military jets could be heard. Many hoped that this would unite us, that the US would become a leader for a new kind of response, a recognition of what was being said in such an attack, using the World Court and diplomacy – but no. The US government chose to see it as a "Pearl Harbor" event – an attack on US soil that gave us permission to attack our attacker – and decided that a Saudi prince, Osama bin Laden (whose family members were the only people allowed to leave the US immediately after the attack), and his band of militant Muslims was responsible for this crime, that they were being supported by Iraq and housed in Afghanistan, and that therefore the US should invade Iraq and Afghanistan. Again, the world was stunned, not expecting, nor really understanding, this choice of actions.

And so the ongoing war in the Middle East that has defined much of the 21st century so far, was launched. Thousands of young men and women, from the dozen or so countries who count themselves allies of the US, went into the villages and towns across unfamiliar lands seeking out militant Muslim guerilla fighters. At first it seemed that a violent regime might be replaced by an American-style democracy and many were hopeful, but centuries-old patterns of warlords and strong-man rule could not be overturned in a few weeks, or months, or even years – especially when the invaders were non-Muslim infidels and too often injured innocent civilians in their efforts. Their hopes were dashed and many were disappointed, then angry, and finally resentful of the constant presence of uniformed soldiers who did not speak their language or understand their ways.

That war was, in part, an attempt to bolster the increasingly intertwined, but then somewhat stagnant, economies of the US and the European Union. History had shown that wars meant increased spending by governments and their after-math led to increased spending by returning soldiers and their families. And spending meant consumption of products which meant profits for producers and what was called a healthy economy.

This time, though, that was not the case. Instead, some of the new products developed by bankers to maximize their corporate profits began to fall apart, and, once more, people who had enjoyed the appearance of great wealth were suddenly impoverished – and often homeless.

They had been sold on going into more and more debt in order to provide for themselves and their families – and that debt soon was greater than their incomes could support.

The Great Recession (called such because we dare not use the accurate term, depression) devastated thousands of businesses and millions of families. And again, the US government responded by spending money it didn't have to pay for people and resources to do all kinds of projects, and to shore up the large banks that they dare not let fail. Hurricane Katrina wiping out a large part of New Orleans, leaving thousands of homeless gathered in totally inadequate shelters, and flooding much of the US Gulf coast with crude oil, was a precursor to the financial breakdown that simply highlighted the multiple issues of the time.

THE 2010S

By 2010 the wars in the Middle East had become a steady background beat behind all the other things going on. Much of the US population was still feeling the effects of losing their jobs and their homes. Europe and the rest of the world were still reeling from the impacts of a failed US economy. And the Earth continued to be degraded by the industry, transportation, and now military actions, of humanity. Now temperatures were measurably increasing around the world, so that each year had record highs over any previous year in the past century. Icebergs and glaciers were disappearing. Large areas of oceans were "dead zones." But for the average urban apartment dweller, or suburban family, little of that was evident. They were busy trying to recreate a life that worked, and using ever more sophisticated computing devices to do so.

Over this decade, the cellular phone, once a luxury for the very rich and busy, became an essential part of life and work for everyone above the age of 12. It quickly evolved into the "smart" phone – a handheld computer with more power than any desktop of the 1990s – that tied into the internet and provided its user with access to all the information available through whatever search engine they were using. It also let them share information through specific sites called "social media" – designed to let anyone who signed up with them post online whatever form of information they wished to share, with whoever was willing to look at it. Perhaps more than any other technology, the personal smart phone defined this decade. People all over the world not only talked with friends, family, and colleagues on these devices, but they sent emails, ordered products, navigated roadways, and, by the end of the decade, took pictures and videos that could be instantly shared all over the world.

2020

It's now 2020. All the above issues, problems, and processes continue, but the world has been through another unthinkable event: a voluntary self-quarantine by billions of people because of fear of infection by a new kind of virus.

CoViD-19 (Corona Virus Disease of 2019) emerged suddenly and affected people in such unpredictable ways that it terrified health agencies, so they persuaded governments to shut down businesses, schools, sporting events, and much of transportation in an attempt to prevent its spread and minimize the potential deaths. In March of 2020 it seemed, based on what was happening elsewhere, that as many as 100 million Americans might die from this disease – and no one wanted to be held responsible for that. As it is turning out, the disease has about the same death-rate as the flu viruses that we deal with each year, but health officials remain terrified that it might get out of control and infect millions more. Not surprisingly, again, the fearful thoughts have been expressed everywhere people share their fears: is this Armageddon? Has the Apocalypse begun?

A Different Viewpoint on Past Developments

One way to understand this past century is that humanity has gone from living as relatively isolated islands to becoming a planetary entity. Humanity can now be seen as an electronically-interconnected being, whose cells are individual people, whose organs are businesses and governments, and whose processes are completely intertwined with planetary processes, just as a fetus' processes are intertwined with the mother's. Our electronic and ecological processes have brought us to this point and we are now, with Climate Change, being required to move through the birth canal and, perhaps, even leave the mother's body – heading, as tech-giants Elon Musk and Jeff Bezos have worked toward, for other planets in the system.

Another way to look at what's been happening over the past century is to follow, not the physical and technological developments, but the intellectual and psychological evolution. At the beginning of the 20th century most of the US and Europe defined themselves in terms of a Judeo-Christian model of the world and divinity. Although there were some translations of Hindu, Buddhist, Zoroastrian, and Taoist texts as early as the 1850s, few people were aware of them, much less had read them. Those who had read them were, in those early years of the century, offering a different way to define ourselves, a new set of principles, drawing on the same roots as the Judeo-Christian idea, but extending it as what they called New Thought. Similarly in countries with other religious traditions.

Then the first and second World Wars, and the Great Depression, along with a massive introduction to higher education, led to a totally different understanding of who we must be. Way back in the 16th century Francis Bacon, often called the father of modern science, said that "a little philosophie (the term for science through the 1700s) tends one toward atheism," which has been shown over and over again to be true.

By the mid-20th century church and synagogue attendance was on the decline across Europe and the US, and through the 1970s, India saw reductions in participation in ritual, and now we see it in Muslim countries, as generations live through the realization that the "two masters" of Science and Religion cannot be served: one must choose. If one accepts the teachings of the Abrahamic traditions, or the strict rituals of the Brahmic traditions, one cannot accept the results of the past couple centuries of scientific inquiry. If one accepts the evidence and the methods of the sciences, one cannot accept the strict interpretation of any Western sacred literature nor the reasoning behind much of religious ritual. This is one of the reasons Marx, Lenin, and Engels spoke harshly of religion, leading to the persecution of religious practitioners throughout the Soviet Union and Marxist China.

Now, for some decades, much of humanity – particularly the educated, technically skilled folk in Western nations and Asia – have been inclined toward agnosticism (questioning the nature or reality of any divine power), even atheism (believing there is no divine power), and certainly humanism (believing that we are the only power in our lives; that nothing but our body's biochemistry affects our thinking and actions).

At least through their middle years, that is. For a strange thing happens after one has practiced the sciences, or simply lived life paying attention for that matter, over a few decades: As Bacon went on to say "but when it beholdeth the chain of [events], confederate and linked together, it must needs fly to Providence and Deity." A student of Werner Heisenberg, one of the early quantum physicists, says that he often quoted an old aphorism: "the first sip from the cup of knowledge separates us from God, but at the bottom of the cup God is waiting." And the mid-19th century professor of Natural Sciences and evangelical Christian, Henry Drummond pointed out that "no one can study science without questioning the ideas that they were told were true when they were children."

Looking back into the 20th century with this in mind, we can see that the men in the US who were sent to college after WWII had "a sip of knowledge" then went out into the world to make a living and raise their families. Many of them avoided religion during their children's formative years, which was also the height of humanism in the US; then a few of them – often through addiction recovery processes – discovered a higher power working in their lives in their middle and elder years. Their Baby-boomer children were sent to under-staffed colleges where they were often taught by young instructors who, themselves had "a little philosophie" and not much life experience. As a result most of those young students didn't get to see how it is that a white-haired scientist has usually found "the bottom of the cup" and reconciled a relationship with the divine that is usually quite different from the one they were taught growing up.

This upbringing meant that the Baby-boomers were given the message that a humanist approach was logical while a religious approach was traditional and probably useless, then were left on their own. Over time, as typically happens, they began to discover the fact that paying attention to life and work – finding the "bottom of the cup" in whatever study one is focused on – leads one to accept the necessity of a greater-than-human source of the order and harmony one experiences.

It's not too surprising then, that in the US Baby-boomers approaching their elder years have become enamored of what has been called New Age Spirituality. Feeling the need for a "Providence and Deity" they were aware that neither the traditional religious teachings nor the humanist leanings of their childhood fit what they've experienced, while the broader precepts and understandings of "New Age Spirituality" make sense to them.

Equally unsurprisingly, a similar process has occurred in other countries, as well.

Around the world the Babyboomers' children, the X and Y generations, and their grandchildren, the Millennials, have, with few exceptions (usually among fundamentalist families who have restricted their childrens' contact with the rest of the world) grown up in a heterogeneous environment where they hear and read and see virtually all of the ways of thinking that are floating around the world, today.

Unlike children growing up prior to WWII, these young people didn't have a clear Judeo-Christian (or Hindu or Muslim or...) source for their spiritual base. Unlike the Babyboomers, they didn't have a strong humanist base with a weak religious input when they were growing up. As a result, each of the successive generations has been given less and less to draw on from childhood, and more and more options in the world around them.

Over the years this has led to increasing despair among successive generations of adolescents (what can I rebel against? What direction can I choose that is really mine?), and to more and more adamant determination to choose a path and follow it among young adults. Lacking a base to build on – and rebel against – each generation is either more lost in over-choice (a term coined by futurist Alvin Toffler in the 1970s) or more fervently attached to what they do choose, than the previous

Lacking a base to build on – and rebel against – each generation is either more lost in over-choice (a term coined by futurist Alvin Toffler in the 1970s) or more fervently attached to what they do choose, than the previous.

Looking at the past few decades in this way, it's clear that humanity as a whole has been lifting veil after veil after veil, and discovering a very different world each time. From the recognition that our material stuff is not really solid, to the realization that our actions have an impact on the natural world around us, to the constantly changing threat of world destruction through use of weapons and the experience of instantaneous communication with people from all ways of thinking and walks of life, we have been com-

pelled to see more and more clearly who we are
and what we are part of. But there's more...

2020 Waves & Visions

Perusing social media it's been impossible to miss what is becoming a flood of descriptions of dreams, visions, and Near-Death Experiences (NDEs). In these Apocalyptic experiences Jesus the Nazarene is telling people to pray for Donald Trump and his associates in order to turn around a potential disaster that is expected this fall: a new wave of distress and with it, a heavy-handed military presence eliminating our freedoms – going beyond the methods that were tested and proven effective this past spring.

What is being said in all these presentations is disturbing, but there is a sincere desire in them and they hold a kernel of a much deeper process that's going on.

The Key to the Issues

That the US has been emotionally divided is very much in our awareness these days, and it's not new, though it was not believed to be the case among light-skinned Americans until Nixon called on "the silent majority" to get him elected in 1968. That the emotional division tends to follow religious lines is also not new: the "religious right" (literally-interpreting Bible-based Christians) has been increasingly vocal in their opposition to the "secular humanists" and "liberals" of mainstream politics, education, and media since Newt Gingrich ran Congress in the

1990s. That's when the tradition of treating one's fellow lawmakers as gentlemen and ladies, and the president with honor and respect, began to fall apart and raw emotions began to be publicized in the media. The fact that many leaders of the "religious right" have since been working hard to bring about their understanding of what the New Testament Book of Revelation describes through a huge battle over Israel is not so well understood, but it's been a powerful political influence for decades.

At this moment, it appears that the trigger issue for the "religious right" is a Supreme Court decision, made in the 1970s, that said a woman had the right to choose to have an abortion legally, in a medical facility. Known as Roe v. Wade, that decision recognized that because they were denied that right women were dying unnecessarily from unsanitary procedures, simply because they couldn't face – for social, economic, or medical reasons – having a child at a particular time in their lives. The Court used the Constitution and the medical opinion of the time – that an unborn fetus did not have feelings or awareness – as the basis of its decision.

The "right to choose" became a feminist issue: women wanted more power in the culture than was acceptable prior to the 1970s and this ability to make their own decisions about their bodies and their lives seemed pretty basic. The "right to life" became the opposing view, stating that God caused the child to be conceived and so it was a living soul from the moment of con-

ception.[1] The fact that the same people were per-
fectly willing to kill a criminal or send soldiers
off to war didn't seem to them to be a conflict –
in their minds adults could make decisions
about their lives for which they might pay the
price of death, but innocents in the womb could
not and should not be killed simply because
they were unwanted.

In the last couple of decades – since 9/11, in
fact – the idea has emerged among the "religious
right" that the US is cursed because of that decision, that because the government supports
the "murder of unborn children" whom God has
placed in the womb, everything else that the US
stands for in the world is besmirched and beginning to crumble. They have come to believe
that, unless and until that decision is reversed
and the government no longer condones, much
less supports, abortion, this country is going to
continue to fall apart and become subject to evil
powers seeking total domination and control.

Really. This is the fear that is driving this
group of people. And it borders on terror.

So, in their minds any woman who seeks any
kind of power, any medical person or agency
who ever assists in aborting a fetus, any activist

---

[1] It's worth noting that this led to vast research into
what the fetal experience actually is, and ultimately
changed the prevailing medical opinion, so that now it's
understood that a fetus has all the requirements for being
human somewhere in the second trimester, and may be
aware before then.

who seeks gender equality in the workplace or in schools, and any politician who supports any of the above, is helping to destroy the US and bring horrifying evil into the land.

The Politics

Understanding the perceived issue, the whole political scene of the past couple decades begins to make sense. Because Newt Gingrich helped launch the "religious right" as a political presence in the 1990s and continues to strongly influence the Republican party, everything that party does is designed to accomplish one thing: keep Republicans in power in order to overturn the Roe v. Wade decision. Because the Democrats stand for equal rights and the empowerment of all genders, races, creeds, and orientations, they must uphold the "right to choose." Because historically, Republicans have stood for free markets and the ability of individuals to make their way in the world, and they portray Democrats as socialists who want the federal government to control everything and manage peoples' lives in an effort to ensure their needs are met, wealthy and upwardly mobile folks who don't care about Roe v. Wade get brought along and support the Republican effort.

So when Democrats are in office, they're portrayed by both the "religious right" and the upwardly mobile and wealthy members of the Republican party as evil beings who are undermining everything that the US stands for – continuing to use the language that Newt Gingrich taught the party to use in the '90s against every opponent, regardless of policy or person.

When Republicans are in office and they've taken the pledge to undo Roe v. Wade and stop the federal government's funding of "socialist" programs, they're given a free ride, with full support from the party. "Whatever it takes to get the job done" is the understanding. The result has been a deepening divide and increasing unwillingness to listen to any other policy stands. A single issue, combined with hateful language and strong innuendo, has transformed the US legislature from a mutually respectful, though differing, body of thoughtful, caring people to a painful, difficult process for everyone, on both sides of the aisle.

The Visions

The recent explosion of reports of dreams, visions, and NDE guidance is happening across the country, underlines this political, social, and religious context. Driven by the fears and anxieties induced by the CoVid-19 pandemic and shaped by the issues described above, religious and spiritual people all over the world are having visions and dreams, and publishing their experiences on the social media, particularly YouTube.

They're all being told in multiple ways that another wave of distress is coming this fall, and that it could be worse than what we've been through. Many are being encouraged to deepen

their spiritual practice and stock up on supplies
to minimize its effects.

Bible-based Christians are getting a very
clear political message as well:

- They're being told that Donald Trump's
  election stopped a political and economic
  plan that is designed to enslave all Americans in a dark future that will enable a
  very few powerful people to live well and
  free.
- They're being told that we've been through
  one and more waves of distress are coming
  (some say a third one is on the way; some
  say 2 more); with the radical shift in political and social expression after the 2018
  election being 1 wave of disruption; the
  CoVid-19 pandemic a second and the on-
  coming flu season with possibly a new
  strain could be another, as could violent
  reactions to the elections being met with
  military force.
- They're being told that "Trump is turning
  people to God" and needs their prayers to
  continue to do this important work.
- They're being told to earnestly pray for
  Trump and his Attorney General, Bill
  Barr, to put an end to the evil and corruption that has, for years, been everywhere
  in the media and government.
- They're being told that undoing Roe v.
  Wade will return America to its blessed
  state.

- They're being told that the passionate action of members of Jesus' Church is the only thing between humanity's glory and its degradation into slavery.

To address all this they're being encouraged in these visions to do four things:

1. Pray for the current leaders of the nation;
2. Let go of any tendencies to turn away from Jesus' teachings, including the belief that individuals can do anything without divine support;
3. Stock up on essentials to help those who will be in need as the next wave of distress hits;
4. Vote in the November election for the people who will undo Roe v. Wade.

And, having accepted that a literally interpreted authority outside themselves must be paid attention to, they have accepted these images and instructions at face value and are sharing them with the world.

The Meaning

Listening, observing, noting consistencies and differences, and comparing these images with other sources of information and, finally, going inside to find my own spiritual guidance, has not been easy. Some of it hasn't been pleasant, but there is in all of this a deeper understanding that can guide us all. The key is in the interpretation of the visions and dreams.

LEVEL ONE – THE SURFACE

The first level of meaning is, always, the literal one – taking things at face value and seeing where they go. In this case, it's pretty clear, beyond the religious framework, these visions are saying that

- CoVid-19 and a larger wave of distress that follows it will determine the future of humanity.
- Be prepared to see many people suffer and to help them as those waves come, probably this fall.
- Trump's election stopped a political/economic process toward control and domination that was unfolding and can't proceed while he's in office.
- There is a long history of corruption in the US government and in the media that is on the verge of getting dismantled.
- The way to effect change in the world is to pray and in government is to vote.

Very straightforward, and not much new, except the idea that the outsider Trump being elected meant that the unfolding political/economic processes on Capitol Hill (along with New York City) came to a screeching halt. What that agenda is hasn't become clear, but the images in the visions range from robots ruling the world to a few people living in highly guarded compounds while the rest of us live in deplorable conditions producing what they want for their comfort – both of which are straight out of the science fiction of the 1950s and '60s.

Yet there's a note of reality in them worth exploring. Analyzing the direction of legislation and executive orders over the past several decades from this perspective it becomes clear that there is a pattern of eroding freedoms and increasing control by the federal government. There are also several mechanisms in place supporting large companies "too big to fail" and individuals of great wealth to keep that wealth. Some examples include increased federal involvement in education and healthcare, restrictions on businesses made in the name of environmental protection and safety, and laws imposing federal standards on local governments, while large banks, utilities, and food producers are subsidized and few if any taxes are paid by the very wealthy. The federalization of the states' National Guard troops and their increased use outside of their states is another indicator. It would be possible to project, based on those trends and current communication systems, that the rights of states and local governments could be almost completely eradicated fairly quickly and federal-based enforcers could be put in place – which of course, is what we've seen hints of in the lockdown and the post-lockdown protests. Whether intentional or not, there is a strong tendency toward the centralization of power and the support of a few, wealthy individuals and companies.

Could this be what Trump is said to be stopping? It doesn't look like it from the outside, noting what he has signed and what Congress has

passed while he's been in office. Many of those
actions seem to be to consolidate and even en-
hance power in the Executive branch of the US
government. So is there something else?

There is another trend unfolding, which
could be what they're seeing in their visions. It's
not a governmental process, and it's not Artifi-
cial Intelligence taking over the world (which is
not physically possible for the foreseeable future), but a media-managed process. Since the
1970s the US has shifted from a cash-based
economy to a debt-based economy – at every level. Not only does the government run on bor-
rowed money, many people think that's the only
way to run a business, and, with home mortgag-
es and credit cards, many more don't know any
other way to run their lives. It's media-managed
because all of the consumer debt is a function of
the advertising that encourages people to think
they must buy things now and that a credit card
exists to make that possible. That, plus the in-
sistence on college-tuition loans and the belief
that one must have health insurance to survive
in this world, has caused far too many people to
become "slaves" to the job market, taking whatever job they can get into and keeping it, regardless of the cost to their personal lives, in order to
pay their debts and have insurance to pay for
the damage they're doing to their bodies. Perhaps this is the slavery the visions are present-
ing? If so, it's not clear how Trump becoming
President has put a roadblock in that process,
except that he's a wild card and no one knows

which way he'll jump. In either case, the future they're terrified of does seem to have roots in the current situation,

As for the waves of disruption, it could be the pandemic and more like it, or it could be a disruption in thought and feeling: the reaction (both for and against Trump) being the first, the upsets and shifts in values resulting from the lockdown being a second, and a deeper awakening/upset emerging this fall could be the third. It could also be natural processes: the multitude of tropical and unseasonal storms; tsunamis wiping out cities; windstorms wiping out crops; heat waves and forest fires wiping out communities. Finally, it could actually be waves of invasions: Russian and Chinese intervention in our elections and economy could be wave one; Chinese economic pressure through trade wars and Russian-created vaccines could be wave two; with an actual physical takeover of the US by one or both as the third/fourth. That would be terrifying, for sure!

Then, there's the corruption in government and media. This could go either direction: corruption among those who support the Republican agenda or corruption among those who support the Democratic agenda, or, ideally, the realization that the whole system has become corrupt as fewer and fewer people have more and more power and wealth, leaving America impoverished. Interestingly, what's being envisioned could be a physical, rather than legal corruption – literally parts of the body failing and falling apart – in both government and the whole media/ entertainment industry as new technologies emerge and shifts in values occur. Or it could be the realization that debt and advertising are no way to maintain a healthy economy and have corrupted both government and the media/entertainment industry in ways that have damaged millions of lives for far too long.

Praying and voting as the ways to respond are interesting, because from all appearances, that's no news: it's what the "religious right" has been doing since the '90s. What appears to be different in these visions is the reminder of what effective prayer really is.[2] People are being told to "enter the secret place" to "command" and "be passionate", and to pray for the Trump administration's people whether they like them or not. They're being told that this is not the kind of thing one does on Sunday in church but what one does when one desperately longs for something, and is determined to bring it about. Then they're being told to go out and share what they've learned and get people to actively take a stand against the evil that is threatening to overcome the country, through their power to vote.

---

[2] If you're interested in more of my thoughts on that subject, and some guidelines for how prayer, in any spiritual tradition, works, see my book *Uncommon Prayer*.

LEVEL TWO – THE CULTURAL SYMBOLS

The second level of meaning looks behind the surface at what the images might stand for in the world. Considering them from this perspective we see a wide range of possibilities, some or all of which could be true.

- A vision of takeover of the US by an enemy foreign power was unfolding using people in the existing power structure to bring it about;
  - o An oligarchy was increasingly controlling the US government and eliminating the power of the vote so that citizens no longer choose their representatives as federal control over their lives increases;
  - o Mind-control through the media and internet or other technologies, directing the emotional state and thought processes of the population was becoming more and more effective;
  - o Deeper attachment to material things was increasingly preventing the spirit's freedom.
- A vision in which Trump's election stopped that process and his presence in office prevents it, symbolically could be:
  - o An outsider is technically in charge and simply not playing the game, so the collective's power to move an agenda is on hold
  - o A big blonde brash heroic figure believed to have been highly successful stopped whatever people were thinking

and doing about politics by showing up
and doing what he thinks is right, regardless.

- o An upset of expectations and regular
  use of brash, strong language opened
  up hidden wounds so the enslaving
  tendency to overlook issues and cover
  them up is no longer happening.
- o Humanity's tendency to allow others to
  tell us what to do has allowed us to
  sink into a form of enslavement but the
  rise of someone who clearly uses his
  personal power to get what he wants
  has reversed the underlying assumptions.

- A vision of waves of disruption where one
  has occurred and another, bigger one is on
  the way (some say a third one is on the way;
  some say 2 more), symbolically could be:
  - o Waves are often emotions – we've been
    through 2 emotional upsets and there
    are one or two more to come, even more
    intense
  - o Disruption and distress are like waves
    on an ocean – you can fight them, go
    through them, or ride them into shore –
    so pay attention to what didn't work
    and be prepared to do something dif-
    ferent in the months ahead.
  - o Waves of transformation, like tsuna-
    mis, clear away the past to allow some-
    thing new to be built: what was normal
    no longer serves and is being wiped

away in waves – we've been through at least one and can expect more.

- A vision that long-term corruption in the government and the media is about to be disclosed and dealt with, symbolically could be:
  - o We all have infections and corruptions in our families, bodies, and souls, as we've compromised our integrity or allowed an idea that is contrary to our ideals take root in our minds – the government of our being – and language – the media of our being; this may be the time we acknowledge and cleanse those
  - o Our nation's refusal to acknowledge the negative impacts our actions have on the natural world around us is a form of corruption – maintained by both media and government – and we may be required to see and deal with that.
- Guidance that the way to address these issues and mitigate the distress is to pray and vote is a reminder that:
  - o Every action is both inner and outer.
  - o Prayer brings us into alignment with a deeper plan for our lives, so shift from looking for outward solutions and go inward.
  - o Connecting with power is essential for accomplishing change – both internally and externally
  - o Humanity has been given the power to choose, and to call forth in this world what our heart's desire, so use it.

LEVEL THREE – THE PERSONAL MESSAGE

Every dream and vision is built on an individual's personal symbolic "dictionary." The images offered in anyone's dream or vision have meaning to the person experiencing them, and this is the case for the people reporting theirs in social media, as well. For example, one vision reported on YouTube was of an eagle soaring in the sky and landing on a nest with eggs, then pecking an egg open and pecking the unhatched eaglet to death. The dreamer assumed it was a reference to abortion, but I might have seen it as referring to the dreams and hopes of America (the eagle) being destroyed before coming into full being.

I can't decide for them what their symbols mean to them, but they are now in my experience so I must ask - and here's where the real work begins - what are these symbols pointing to in my own psyche? For whatever we perceive, whether it be with our physical senses or our inner ones, the experience is shaped by the mental framework – the beliefs, assumptions, and expectations – that we hold in the moment. Clearly, for these messages to enter into my awareness, I must have some place in my mental framework that allows for them. And the same is true for all of us. So...

What does Donald Trump's election mean, and how is it disrupting an ongoing process of degradation in my own self? To answer this I need to ask a few questions:

- Was I in a process of disempowering myself that needed to be stopped?
- Do I have an image of a hero as brash, blonde, larger-than-life?
- What processes in me have stopped because of my experience of things like that election?
- What does the US President stand for in my personal life?

What do these waves mean in my life?

- Are they waves of transformation clearing away past beliefs and patterns to allow something new to be built in my soul, my character?
- Are they something for me to struggle against, swim through, or ride – or is each one different, addressing a different aspect of my being and requiring a different strategy?

What kind of corruption is there in my psyche?

- What sort of infectious ideas or attachments do I need to clean out?
- Is my language and communication corrupt?
- Am I governed by my highest ideals or the compromises I've made?

How am I addressing the issues I learn about?

- I have been enfranchised to act; am I truly using my power?
- How is my prayer life – am I entering "the secret space" and passionately insisting on the world I yearn for?

- Am I expressing what I think is important in the world around me? Am I contributing to the collective decision process or am I hiding out in the belief that it doesn't matter what I do or say?

Answering these questions is not trivial. It's a process that may take several days or even weeks to go through. But answer them we must, because we are in a worldwide apocalypse and the veil must be lifted if we are to keep moving forward and not succumb to the fears and distress that are emerging around us along the way.

The Veil Being Lifted Now

There is an old, old saying from the British Isles, "the veil is thin." It's usually said around the time of year we call Hallowe'en, when the days are warm but the nights are cold and getting longer, when the trees and many of the plants have lost their leaves and appear to have died, when a few lights, scattered across the countryside, are all people have to guide them home. There is a sense at that time of year that the veil between life an death, between the material world and spirit world, is thinner than usual, and that we material beings may find ourselves having a spiritual experience on such a night.

Another ancient phrase is "beyond the veil." This usually refers to something that is beyond knowing, beyond our ability to understand. Sometimes it's used to refer to someone who has died, has passed "beyond the veil" that separates the material from the spiritual.

People who are well-read in the Christian tradition will recognize the phrase "rending the veil." The reference is to the curtain that hung in front of the Holy of Holies in the Jerusalem temple which, according to the New Testament, was "rent from top to bottom" when Jesus the Nazarene died on the cross. Several levels of meaning can be found here. First, the screen separating humanity from deity was destroyed. Second, it was destroyed in place, without a human doing it. Third, the tear was from the top, where it was attached, not from the bottom where it was loose, which would be almost impossible to accomplish. Each of these leads to a deeper, richer interpretation of the meaning and importance of that crucifixion.

Then, as described in the Introduction, the word apocalypse, in Greek, means to "lift the veil" of the bride and discover who one will be with for the duration of the marriage.

In all these uses, "the veil" is that which separates the seer from what would be seen. The first two are metaphysical, beyond the physical-material experience, and the last two are physical.

Recently, we've seen, for all the reasons described in the previous section, a renewed interest in the separation between material-physical reality and the spiritual. Television mediums speak to people "beyond the veil" and provide insights and information that are amazing in their accuracy. Teachings abound, in books and online, that are said to be channeled from an entity, or group of entities, who are "beyond the veil" and offer suggestions for how the universe really works and how we can live in it joyfully. In books and on YouTubes and other social media, people of all spiritual traditions are reporting having seen angels and light beings, and many are experiencing the presence of spiritual teachers and saints – even from a tradition that is not their own! Even more are reporting the dreams and visions described earlier in this text.

So what is this veil? What does it do? What does it matter?

The Structure of Things

From the sciences we have learned that the world is not solid, that the spaces between the molecules, atoms, and subatomic elements of an apparently solid object are far greater than the size of the particles that compose it. We also have learned that it seems solid to us because our perceptual system works in a way that perceives the whole as a whole and not as its parts. We've learned, too, that everything is in constant change, moving from one state to another. And we've learned that there is a marvelous underlying order and harmony in that constant change and that our very existence is a function of that harmonious process. Finally, we see that the creative activity and process move forward from a realm that is not in space and time but affects all of space and time, and that all of the elements that make up what appears to be solid around us are drawn together to do so by one unifying force that pervades all space and time.

From the core teachings of all the major religions we learn that there is one essential being that is constantly creating the universe and the individuals within it, guiding their process as they move through a plan for them individually as part of a whole. We learn that this essential being is outside of our normal space and time and yet everywhere in it, and that it works through one, unifying force, called, in English, grace or love. We learn that, while our normal mode of being has prevented us from perceiving this creative essence, it is possible to overcome that normality and enter into a relationship with the source of all.

Both understandings tell us that what is happening *to* us is coming from something that is everywhere – in us, around us, and through us.

Both understandings tell us that what is unfolding in our lives is purposeful, part of something larger that we are part of.

Both understandings say that there is a unifying force moving in and through us and all that is.

A Step Beyond

What religion offers, though, that the sciences do not, is the possibility of relationship beyond the physical-material interactions of our bodies – relationship with other forms of being, and with the source of the power that creates and maintains all that is. This is what the Hebrew bible Psalms and stories of Elijah and Elisha point to. This is what the New Testament, including the rending of the veil and John's Revelation, describes. This is what makes the Bhagavad-Gita and the Q'uran so important. This is what a prophet is demonstrating. This is what visions of angels, saints, and divine beings exemplify.

It's also what some famous elder scientists of the 20th century lived for: Albert Einstein, Carl Jung, Roger Penrose, being the most notable of these. For, in fact, a deep relationship with the source and sustaining presence of all is the next step beyond deep practice of the sciences. Once one has seen and tested and explored the limits of material knowledge for a few decades, one realizes those limits continue to expand and *they will never lead to the fulfillment, the ultimate "why" that is being sought.*

So, we have a choice: either accept that there is a mystery, a veil, beyond which we can never see or know, or continue to explore, using the means and methods of the sciences to penetrate that veil.

What means and methods? The familiar scientific method, of course: observe; question; hypothesize; test; compare and analyze; then reiterate. This is a proven path for acquiring knowledge one can rely on. The difference is, we don't apply it to what one can perceive with the senses, but what one observes with inner awareness.

Why? Because if that which we seek is everywhere present, including within our bodies and awareness, and if focusing on the material world is endless and perhaps fruitless, then it behooves us to apply the method that we know works in another direction.

How? Well, we can start from scratch – and most of us do – or we can do what we were taught in school and do our literature search first to find who's done similar work and build on it, refining that work to meet our particular focus.

And it turns out there are huge bodies of literature to explore. Some of the work is relatively modern, and actually builds a bridge between the material sciences and what, for lack of a better term, may be called the spiritual sciences. Among these are the works published and promoted by the Institute of Noetic Sciences (noetic.org), the Arizona Laboratory for Advances in Consciousness and Health (lach.arizona.edu), and the Science and Nonduality conferences (scienceandnonduality.com). Also, more than one physicist or theoretical mathematician has taken on the problem, perhaps the most powerful attempt being written by a US professor of quantum mechanics, Amit Goswami: *Physics of the Soul.* Some of the literature may be in the realm of "psychical research" and has been published by societies of that name in the US and the UK for over a century. Some of it may be found in the literature of Hebrew and Christian mystics; also the Sufis. The bulk of such literature, however, is to be found in the several thousand-year-old tradition of Tibetan Buddhists, who have developed a highly sophisticated methodology for developing inner awareness, focusing it, and exploring where it takes them. They, in turn, have built on the work of Hindu yogis (using but by no means limited to the body postures, or *asanas*, of *hatha* yoga), as laid out in the aphorisms of Patanjali, written some

2,400 years ago. And, if we could translate meaningfully the writings of the Egyptians, the Mayans, and the Aztecs we would probably discover even more guidelines for such explorations there, as well.

For it turns out that this is not a new problem. In fact, it seems to be as old as civilization. Because of the materialistic focus of life in city-based, Empire-building cultures, much of one's life must be dealing with the material world. But for the enquiring mind, that cannot satisfy. So there has always been a need to go beyond – and, having found a path, the need to share it.

Not Between Two Worlds

When we talk about someone who has died as having gone "beyond the veil" or possibly living "on the other side of the veil," we are implying, and probably assuming, that the world we live in with these material-physical bodies is a world unto itself and that, somewhere, somehow, there is another world, the one where those who live without their bodies are located.

For some, that other world isn't on this planet and so must be somewhere "out there" in the heavens. This is consistent with the narrative of the Abrahamic traditions, as well as some teachings among Buddhists and Hindus (and the other Brahmanic traditions) as well as many indigenous traditions around the world.

For some, that other world may be on this planet, but there's a kind of curtain, like a force field, that keeps us separate. This fits with some shamanic traditions, including neo-Wicca.

For a very few, that other world is here, all around us, but we aren't usually able to perceive it, because we're so attuned to material-physical experience. These people might talk of vibrations or frequency or inter-dimensional experience, saying that the "spirit world" is operating at a higher frequency than our physical senses can tune in to. Several "channeled" works, including the Seth material, support this understanding

Some say all of the above: each planet has spirit beings living on it but they can't be measured by our physical senses or equipment because the physical equipment and senses are operating at such a low, dense, frequency. Edgar Cayce used to talk about how people would leave their bodies when they died and go to the planet that would take them to their next level of understanding (warriors would go to Mars, authoritarian leaders would go to Jupiter, and so on).

Applying the principles that both science and religion tell us, one possibly safe operating assumption in exploring beyond the veil is that the same processes are unfolding and the same force is at work in both forms of being. Since those who are dwelling on "this side" and those on the "other side" have in common the experience of living here, on this planet, as and among other people, we have reason to believe that some elements of life here and life "there" might be the same.

There's much more, however, to the world we call "spiritual" than simply what happens to people who continue to live on past the death of their physical-material body. Most indigenous peoples are aware of wisdom and emotions in the plants, animals, and even rocks and rivers, around them; the shaman's job is to keep that awareness open and maintain balance and harmony among them and with the people.

Many cultures have stories of sprites, brownies, faeries, devas, or other living entities who appear as mostly light or do not take physical form except through the forms of a particular plant or body of water that they energize and experience through.

People who have mystical experiences, in whatever religious tradition (and some with no religious background) are uniform in describing a life, love, and wisdom that is everywhere, in everything, including themselves as part of all of it.

In several North American indigenous cultures, each individual animal or plant is considered a temporary embodiment of its principle being - Coyote, Raven, etc. – which dwells in the Spirit World and becomes manifest in alignment with the will of the Creator, an overarching, great Spirit whose will is the well-being of all.

Exploring

With so many variations, so many descriptions and interpretations, where does one start?

Usually, following the scientific method, one finds the commonalities, the patterns, the consistencies, then notes the inconsistencies, the breaks in the pattern, and the openings. That's where the observation that leads to the hypothesis may be found. This is what a Scottish professor of natural history, Henry Drummond, did in the 1850s, following the principles of the natural sciences into the spiritual world.[3] It's what Thomas Troward did in his books written between 1902 and 1915. A British judge who served in the Punjab, India, for several decades, Troward used the understandings of the time regarding electricity, radio waves, and other forms of vibration to lay out a continuum within which thought could be seen to have power beyond the normal limits of space and time, and then to define the characteristics of a universal thought process and its source.[4] This is also what a number of members of the British (and American) Society for Psychical Research have done, attempting to explain phenomena that were beyond the capacity of current physics and biology. Many independent researchers and

---

[3] Drummond's book, *Natural Law in the Spiritual World*, was a classic for many decades; my interpretation of it, *One Law,* was published as part of the Library of Hidden Knowledge by Beyond Words/Simon & Schuster in 2017.

[4] Several of Troward's books are still in print. My interpretation of his key essays is called *The Power of Creative Thought*, published by Portal Center Press in 2020.

scholars have done the same and published their work online and in books, some of which is reported on the syndicated radio program *Coast-to-Coast AM,* (also online and broadcast around the world), which is dedicated to exploring the edges of traditional science and explorations "beyond the veil."

The Institute of Noetic Sciences has, perhaps, been the most rigorously scientific in their research. And, over several decades now, they've consistently come up with statistically verifiable results demonstrating that people do have aspects of their minds and bodies that work outside our normal understandings of physics and biology.

Reviewing the work that has been done by all these groups and individuals, two things become clear:

(1) that there really are phenomena with consistent characteristics and processes that do occur outside the realm of our current understandings of physics and biology; and

(2) experiences of such phenomena seem to be as much a function of the people in the location as any other characteristics.

This last point is not to say that only certain people perceive what's happening, but to say that others perceive them, as well, when those people are present. A recent example is apparitions of the figure of Mary, the divine mother of Jesus the Nazarene – which only some people see with their eyes or hear, but many people become aware of through other senses – in both Christian and non-Christian countries around the globe.

Beyond these, it is evident that some phenomena are consistent across cultures, as well, with different names and stories in different cultures and language groups. One example of this is the "plant deva' or "faerie." These entities are well known in India and among the Celtic peoples, and a garden in Findhorn, Scotland became quite famous in the 1970s for the size of produce which resulted from reported communications with such beings. Another is what Americans generally call "small greys" and consider to be interplanetary travelers, but which fit almost exactly the descriptions of "brownies", "sprites", and "gnomes" in various countries across Europe.

Putting these ideas together, it appears that there are, in fact, forms of being that share this world but that only some of us are able to perceive, or to create the space for others to perceive. Then the question becomes, if it's possible for some people to perceive them, even occasionally, what makes it possible for them to do so?

The traditional answer is that in some places, at some times, "the veil is thinner" than at others, so we are seeing into the "other world" or they have wandered into ours. The difficulty with that is, if it were so then anyone could see such things in those times and places.

And that's the crux. If what we're calling the veil were some kind of barrier or container, its opening would be seen and felt by everyone in the area. But that doesn't appear to be the case. Instead, it seems that only some people are able to perceive – and they are only able to sense the presence of some kinds of beings, sometimes. There are people who see, and make it possible for others to see plant devas or faeries. Others see angels. Others have regular visits with one or another form of deity.

What seems to matter is not whether there are beings present at a given point in space and time, but whether there is a resonance between the beings and the one seeking to perceive them. In the same way that some animals know if we're friendly or not, apparently spirit beings (or "elementals" as some groups call them) respond similarly. Only if a person's psyche (their emo-tional-spiritual-psychological state) is attuned with theirs can they be seen.

And it turns out that, for most of the folks who see them, it's not with their outer senses, but with their inner senses, that they experience the presence of the other beings.

Inner senses? These are the forms of inner awareness that match our outer senses. If you close your eyes and remember the taste of you most recent meal, for example, you are using your inner sense of taste. If you remember what your bedroom looks like and really let your mind take in the colors and textures and shapes, then you're using your inner vision. Remote viewers who, given a set of coordinates for a location, are able to describe what is there without having been there, are using their inner vision.

If, having trained the mind to distinguish between memory, fantasy, and awareness (which is what Tibetan Buddhist practices are designed to do), one sees or hears a person or other form of being, that is a vision. If it happens more than once, with consistent messages that are in alignment with what science and religion tells us is true about ourselves and the world, then it may be a form of prophecy, or communication with the source of all that is. In either case, it is relationship "beyond the veil."

No, this is not a psychotic episode. (And that assumption demonstrates a consistent problem in this culture-of-control that says anything out of the normal must be an illness.) How to know? First of all, such experiences do not involve the compulsion of the psychotic episode. Second, they are not random or destructive; the perceiver is able to test the information against a set of criteria that both science and religion agree upon. Third, the perceiver has done the preparation work of learning how to discern what is true awareness and what isn't.

Once we have begun to open our inner senses in this way, we need to be able to choose when to do so. It doesn't work to try to function in a physical-material world while sensing the spiritual beings that flow through the same space and time. The apparition of Mary at the town of Medjugorje in Bosnia-Herzegovina has consistently appeared on the second day of the month, allowing the one remaining person who can actually see and hear her to go about her regular life. A Tibetan monk or the shaman of an indigenous people will perform certain procedures before going into the state of consciousness in which visions can occur. Remote viewers do so only when asked, and use only a particular format for coordinates. A devout religious practitioner sets a time to enter into communion with the divine.

All of them have learned three things:

1. The difference between memory, illusion, fantasy, and inner awareness
2. How to adjust their consciousness, their psyche, so that it resonates with the beings they intend to perceive
3. When and where, in space and time, is best to do so.

As a result all of them have the capacity to use an inner faculty in the same way they use their outer senses, activating the same areas of the brain and experiencing the same degrees of clarity. They "see", "hear", "taste", "touch" and "smell" internal experiences – or are able to use one or more of those senses – in the same way they do in the outer world. They have simply expanded their abilities beyond what their parents and teachers taught them growing up.

Looking Forward

So what does all this have to do with the Apocalypse?

Everything. If, in truth, lifting the veil is not removing a barrier "out there" but developing an internal ability, then the Apocalypse is the process by which we practice that ability.

More than that, an Apocalypse may be the means by which we accomplish, or fulfill, our life's purpose. There's a common understanding that, through the Apocalypse, the world as we know it comes to an end. This was a major concern during 2012 when some people misinterpreted the Mayan calendar to mean that December 21, 2012 was the "end of the world." The Toltec calendar places the date in 2021.

But what if the "end of the world" is not its death, but its fulfillment? What if the word "end" really means "purpose" or "goal"? If that's the case, then Apocalypse is what we really want – our fulfillment, the achievement of our life's purpose The message of John's Revelation in the Christian New Testament is that at some point the world will no longer experience Heaven and Earth as two separate places, and that those who live in the new "place of peace" (which is what Je-ru-salem means) will be in continual relationship with the creative Source of all that is.

Many people have attempted to understand what John was telling us in his Revelation. A number have pointed out that there appears to be an internal framework to the description that corresponds to the training offered by mystery schools at the time. That training involved the completion of 7 basic studies, followed by an 8th, which focused on the relationship between the constellations in the sky and the events of one's life and the world, and culminated with a 9th level, which involved and required a relationship with the divine. Looking at the book from that perspective, it all makes sense, and the Apocalypse he was describing can be understood as an internal experience, an initiatory progression, starting out at the 7th level, moving through the 8th, and pointing to the 9th, an ongoing relationship with the divine source of all that is.

Using that framework, and with our understanding of what it takes to "lift the veil," getting there may not, after all, be a process of watching some battle happening on the planet. It may require, instead, that we face our own internal demons and cast them out. It may require that we allow ourselves to be guided by a higher truth, and the 7 candlesticks and 7 churches may be our 7 energy centers, affecting our 7 glandular systems and emotional conditions, as ancient Hindu and Buddhist texts suggest.

When today's prophets, all those people having dreams and visions of the coming waves of distress and hearing directions to pray for Trump and the other leaders of the US, they're being told just exactly this. They are being told to let go of past limiting beliefs and practices and really connect with their source and sustainer, passionately insisting that the past evils of the world be cut away so that a new Heaven and a new Earth ("thy will be done on Earth as it is in Heaven") can exist in this world we all share.

John's Armageddon, therefore, may not be the destined battlefield of millions of soldiers, but rather the place inside us where we come to terms with all that keeps us separated from our own self, our beloveds, our neighbors, and our enemies – and hence from the source and sustainer of our being. The number of the beast (666) may not be something that someone brands upon our bodies, but may be the number of times we must turn away from our tendency to degrade ourselves or others with our thoughts, words, or actions. The "whore of Babylon" may not be any city, state, or kingdom, but may be our own attachment to the material things of this world, ready to be replaced by the purity of our true soul's longing: a deep, loving relationship with the source of all we are and all that is.

If the Apocalypse is an internal process leading us from an unfulfilling search for answers and fulfillment in the material world, toward the freedom to live in total harmony with universal processes; if "lifting the veil" means learning to shift our focus from only on what's "out there" in the material-physical world to experience also what's flowing around, through, and in all of us as Spirit; if Revelation is a deep, resonant experience of the loving presence and process that is constantly creating and sustaining all that is – then why wait? Isn't that all that we've always longed for?

Some How-Tos

It's all very well to say that it's time to "lift the veil" and see what's Real behind the appearances, but how do we go about it? There are literally thousands of techniques and guides out there for doing this, but the next few pages introduce some easy processes for getting out of our habitual mindsets and beginning to see clearly beyond the norm.

How We See Things

Most of the time we are using our eyes to see, not what's actually in front of us, but what our minds have decided must be there. Following are some well-known examples:

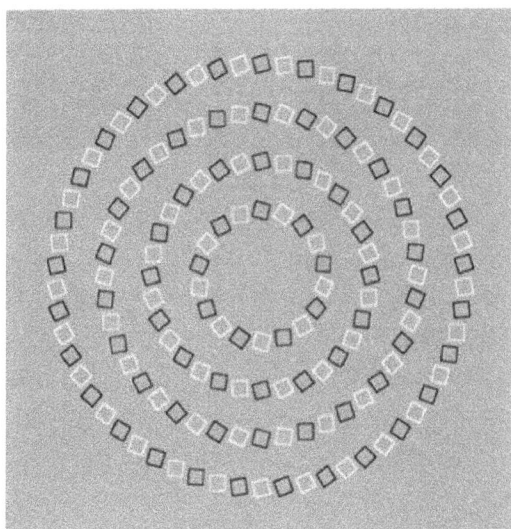

(1) You may have to use your finger to trace these to understand this illustration, or it may be enough for you to focus on the smallest circle to see that this is not a picture of a spiral but a set of 4 concentric circles. Because of the slight angles of the squares making up the circle, the eye has sent a message to the brain saying it must be a spiral.

(2) Is this an older woman looking down? Or is it a younger woman looking away? Again, it's both, depending on how you interpret the lines you are seeing. The "older woman's" eye is the "younger woman's" ear. The "older woman's" nose is the younger woman's chin. The "older woman's" mouth is the "younger woman's" necklace.

(3) Are there 3 objects or 4? Which end are you looking at? It's actually one continuous form with a different number of shapes at each end.

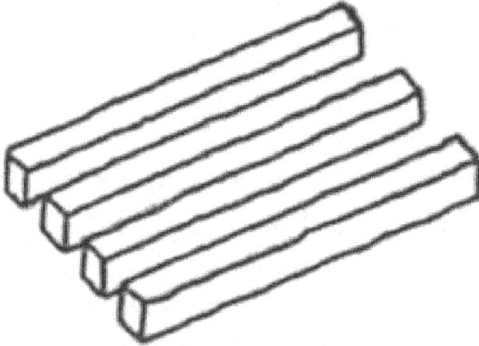

Our minds are designed to discount some things and emphasize others. What's familiar is often totally discounted (like the sound of a refrigerator or air conditioning) while what is strange is often interpreted to be something already known. And, in some cases, the strange thing is dismissed altogether as "impossible, therefore nonexistent."

The last couple decades' work of neurophysiologists and neuropsychologists has helped us understand how this works. It turns out there are at least two factors at play: the neurons in the brain that connect and disconnect with other neurons based on usage ("neurons that fire together wire together"), and a set of cells at the back of the eyeball that whose purpose was not clear until someone demonstrated that they're what send the message to the brain telling it what's being seen and they work like old-fashioned "film strips", sending a pre-existing set of images based on similar past experiences and partial cues being received from the environment.

The great news is none of that is stuck in place – it's all "plastic" and changeable – and Joe Dispenza's books and workshops have helped thousands of people begin to shift the neural networks and pre-existing "filmstrips" to have different kinds of experiences in the future from the ones they've had in the past. He and others offer experiences that open the way for different kinds of perceptions, and encourage the use of "mental movies" to tell the brain to shift to a different set of expectations about who we are and how the world works, so we can see the world around us differently.

The Stories We Tell Ourselves

When we were born we had already had months of experiences in our mother's womb, and these helped to form the early networks in our neurons. The emotions, the music, the food, even the voices around a pregnant woman all affect the way the fetus' brain develops – and sets a pattern for how the child will experience the world. Then, in the world, children experience all kinds of inputs, including messages about what the world "really is," from the people (both physical and electronic) around them. These messages are internalized and become "rules" the child will live from for years, sometimes a whole lifetime, until and unless something happens to demonstrate that those "rules" about how things "have to be" are no longer useful or valid.

Those "rules" are based on the inner narrative that each of us creates about who we are and how the world works, as we go through life. Without that narrative, or story, nothing would make any sense. We'd wake up in the morning and see isolated objects: ceiling, wall, clock, sheets, etc.. Then we'd make a decision about each of those things as we encountered it: shall I turn off the buzzer on clock? Shall I pull the plug or find the button? Shall I lift the sheet off the body? How shall I roll the body over toward edge of bed? And so forth. Each action would require that we recognize the components and then choose what to do with each one as we encounter it. Our inner narrative tells us "It's morning and time to wake up! I'm in my bedroom; good. Now I hit the button on the clock and throw back the sheet and blanket, so I can get up and head to the bathroom..." Sometimes we accompany that story with another one, about how hard it is to get up, or how lovely it is to start a new day, or whatever. And, after a few hundred times, we don't even hear the story, but the body does all these things automatically.

So the story we tell ourselves about our lives and our experiences determines our choices, which then become our automatic, habitual thoughts and behaviors – about everything in our world. Only when we travel to some place new, or spend time with someone who doesn't fit in with our norms do we even begin to see the possibility of a different pattern.

This means that, if you are living in or near where you grew up, spending time (physically or electronically) only with people like you have always known, doing pretty much the same kind of work you always have – you are likely to be going through automatic habits day after day, with few challenges to the "rules" about who you are and how the world works that you made up as a child. Such people often have a very difficult time recognizing that the world could be different from what "it's always been" or that there might be another way of doing things that works as well as or better than what you've "always done."

If, on the other hand, you have lived in different kinds of places, have experienced (physically, electronically, or through reading) different kinds of people who have other understandings of how the world works, and make a point to frequently try new things or learn new ways of doing things, your brain has many more possible connections and far fewer habits built in. This means that you will be far more open to new ways of thinking or doing things, and will be more likely to perceive something that might otherwise have slipped right past you.

So, as we are "lifting the veil" part of what we're doing is taking a look at how our inner narrative about who we are and how the world woks has limited our ability to perceive and understand other peoples' experiences and ways of being.

This is the function of the training that priests, shamans, Tibetan lamas, and other spiritual leaders go through. They're given opportunities to become aware of the stories they have accepted from childhood and give up the "rules" they made then, so they can allow new possibilities and stories to be formed, and be aware that there are many ways to experience this world. From that awareness they can then formulate a new narrative, that includes a much broader range of possibilities than that of the folks around them who are still living from their childhood stories and rules.

In today's world we have access to thousands of books and trainings (physical and electronic) that can help us do the same thing. It helps to have a mentor or guide through the process, because it's easy to get lost in the sea of potentials. Happily, it turns out that the world works in such a way that once we start on this path, generally the right person to show us the next steps will appear ("when the student is ready the teacher appears"). You may have experienced this: you decide you want to learn something, or you sign up for a class, and suddenly books and people show up around you that support that process. It's called "synchronicity," a term coined by Swiss psychotherapist Carl Jung to describe how events related to what we're thinking tend to happen even though we didn't intentionally cause them to happen.

How do we discover our stories, our "rules", our beliefs about ourselves and the world we live in? We look around. We observe our actions and our environments, what pleases us and what causes distress. Generally what pleases us fits our story and what distresses us does not fit with what we think should be.

LETTING THE OLD STORIES GO

How do we change them? It's actually a straightforward process, though there is a short way and a long way to accomplish results. The long way is simply, every time we feel distress because something is not as we believe it should be, we tell ourselves what we really want to be experiencing instead. It's like chipping away at an iceberg. We deal with the visible part a little at a time, while more and more of what was under the surface becomes visible. Slowly but steadily we rewire the neural network so the neurons are no long connecting in the same way and we can now see things and do things differently. This is what Benjamin Franklin described doing for himself in his autobiography. A version of it can be found in my interpretation of James Allen's works, called *As We Think So We Are.*

The short way is to recognize that something we've accepted for a long time has a lot of emotions attached to it and so to give ourselves an opportunity to release those emotions. The release then catapults the system into a new state. I've described the process in some detail in two books: *Empowered Care* and *Making the World*

Go Away. A brief version of the steps goes something like this:

1. **Awareness**—seeing that something (e.g., idea, belief, situation, story, person, behavior) in our experience doesn't fit with what we now know or intend our lives to be.

2. **Acceptance** that this is, in fact, part of our current/past experience (rather than pretending it's not).

3. **Acknowledging** that, while it doesn't at this time fit, it has served a purpose in our lives, if only to bring us to this state of being in this moment.

4. **Expressing** the full range of feelings that come up when we look at it—literally "pushing from" our being, our bodies, our emotional center, our intellect, all the feelings, words, images, thoughts, songs, movements, that are associated with this, through writing, speaking, dancing or other movement, music, pounding on pillows, and other safe modes of expression.

5. **Releasing** all of that—filling a virtual "garbage bag", burning papers, showering, etc. – to let the psyche know that this is no longer a part of our narrative about ourselves and the world. (I like stuffing it all into an imaginary rocket ship and sending it into the sun to be transformed into healing light; one person put it in a hot-air balloon and watched it drift away; others ask angels or divine beings to take it away; a "self-consuming" bag works for some folks, too)

6. **For-giving**—in that internal space of release, telling all the people involved that we've let go of this and no longer hold them responsible for their part in it for us; imagining them in front of us and asking them to release/forgive us for holding/blaming them, and for projecting this state or idea or action onto them out of our own unexamined self; accepting that there is no blame/judgment from "on high" and stepping into a delightful "state of grace" in which "all that exists is the love between you."

7. **Claiming/Declaring**—in that "state of grace" is power, and we focus it to claim/accept a truer idea of our belief/ being/ experience/ relationship.

8. **Affirming**—writing and speaking this new idea frequently, practicing it, and, when any old habits of thought/action are triggered, canceling them and replacing them with this new one.

When we do this kind of process (taking several hours in a quiet space away from folks who might be affected by our activity), we are, to continue the iceberg metaphor, breaking it up into chunks and letting them dissolve and disappear. We use the affirmation as a reminder that we've done this work – and as a signal that there may be a few more chunks that need to be dealt with, should declaring the affirmation not be enough to restore our new level of harmony.

New Stories Mean New Experiences

Applying this to today's world, with all the apocalypses people are experiencing, we can see that it's our attachment to our old ideas of what "should be" or "must be" that is driving far too many of our actions and causing most of our distress. We have allowed ourselves to develop habits of thought and activity that no longer serve us, individually or collectively. So now we take a look at what works and what doesn't work in our lives for the long haul. We get in touch with who we feel we were born to be and what, in our deepest selves, we long to experience. Then we look at how our beliefs about who we are and what is possible in this world helps us or hinders us along that path.

As we let go of the narrative that frames our perceptions and actions, we begin to experience the world very differently. It's not just that we've changed, but it seems that the people around us have changed. In my own experience, letting go of my upset over various financial relationships led to a whole new experience of prosperity – including people paying me without my asking them to. Letting go of my upset over abuse in my childhood led to a very different kind of relationship with, not just my parents, but everyone who had any kind of position of authority over me: without my saying a word to them, they simply didn't act that way anymore. And, in the larger world, I've seen that when I've released old images and fears about violence and harm, my story of what the world is focuses on peace and harmony, and even the news media have different articles! (yes, truly!).

In many ways it is these stories, this narrative, that make up the veil that we must lift during apocalyptic transformations. Our attachment to the decisions we made as children (or in our teens or twenties) makes that veil very thick and heavy, so lifting it seems difficult indeed. But as we allow ourselves to let go of "childish things" of the past we begin to experience a richer life, much less disturbing and distressing, and much more satisfying to our souls.

Connecting With The "Other Side"

In Western, Empire-based culture, children are generally trained, from a very young age, to focus on the material objects and physical bodies around them. If they talk about seeing spirits or "imaginary friends" or any other non-material forms, they're usually told they've been imagining things that aren't real, or, in an enlightened household, they're told "yes, those things exist, but we can't talk about them anywhere else." In worst cases, such things are, as many elderly women have shared with me over the years "beaten out of them."

Not true in other cultures. In fact, among indigenous peoples, such abilities are cultivated as essential contributions to the welfare of the community. For them, knowing what spirit-beings are around and what they intend and are doing is as important as knowing what plants and animals are doing in the natural world.

This difference is because, in the Abrahamic traditions, the activities called "witchcraft" and "fortunetelling" are forbidden in the Hebrew Bible, or Old Testament. But both the Old and New Testament encourage what is called "prophesy," and the New Testament describes "discernment of spirits" as a gift of the Holy Spirit and, unfortunately, most people are very much aware of the former and woefully unaware of the latter, so an important human capacity has been almost totally lost among the Jewish, Christian, and Muslim populations of the world.

To "discern spirits" is to recognize the presence of a form or entity that is not visible to the usual 5 senses. It depends on the use of the "6th sense", often called intuition, or spiritual sight, hearing, smelling, or feeling. Many people have smelled roses when around a spiritual teacher. Others have heard quiet music or a faint tinkling of bells or even a voice when they've entered a state of consciousness that is an experience of peace. A few have maintained, or reclaimed, their childhood ability to be aware when some being is near that is not in a material body; some see its form; others feel its presence. In all these cases there is also the possibility of experiencing words or images that are clearly outside their normal thought patterns and seem to be coming from the being whose presence is felt or seen.

To "prophesy" is, as was explored earlier in this text, to express divine ideas as shared through vision, dream, or direct communication.

This is what charismatic, pentecostal, and evangelical Christians are doing more and more days, which, incidentally, is in accord with the prophesies laid out in the gospel stories of the New Testament.

How do we overcome our childhood training and allow ourselves to use this very human capacity? How do we become aware of the presence of noncorporeal beings? How do we learn to listen to the "Voice of God?"

Because the taboo against doing so is so deeply ingrained in most adults in Western culture, it usually takes either a very long while or a huge event to break down the carefully built up walls against such perceptions and knowings. Many people have been using tools like *A Course in Miracles* or deep meditation for years in this effort. Others have gone through Near Death Experiences or had a calamitous event which shook up their psyches to the point where the walls were broken down.

Happily, the world works in such a way that all of us can benefit from these peoples' efforts and experiences. It turns out that, whenever some entity on the planet changes, all similar entities are more likely to make the same or a similar change. The scientific term is "morphogenetic fields." It means that whenever any of us learns something new, or discovers something, or develops an ability, everyone who thinks or feels or is genetically or socially similar to that person is more able to learn that, discover that, or do that very thing.

So the fact that more people are prophesying, that more people are discerning spirits, that more people are becoming aware of the non-material world that surrounds and interpenetrates this world, means that even more of us are able to do so without near as much effort or nearly so calamitous an event. It means, truly, that we are experiencing a whole new level of "lifting the veil," which, in turn is opening far more people's awareness of what is possible – and what is truly going on in, through, and around us all.

What specific things can we do?

The first thing is to stop censoring our impressions. All teachers of intuition and other non-traditional methods of learning start with this. How can we hear the "still small voice" if we only listen to people who shout? How can we sense the presence of others if we don't allow ourselves to acknowledge the possibility? So, whenever we think maybe there might be something trying to get through, we need to allow it – and write it down. Make it real to our body-minds by putting it into material form.

The next thing is to create opportunities to experience the kind of insights and beings that may be available. Here is where the Old Testament injunction against witchcraft and the New Testament encouragement to discern spirits is an important distinction to make. When we are ego-centered, prideful, or simply intellectually curious, the kinds of intuitive and psychic experiences we have pull us into a darker and more destructive state of consciousness. But when we fill ourselves with love and align ourselves with the highest ideals we can imagine as we go into that way of being, then the experiences can lift us still higher and help all humanity.

Having said that, the possible avenues for such experiences are wide open. Anyone who writes will acknowledge that the writing often happens "through" them rather than by them. Automatic writing, using one's non-dominant hand to allow words to be written on the page, is the next step beyond that. We can simply invite someone to share their wisdom, as Jane Roberts and her husband did, or we can ask for some particular person or presence to assist us, as some spiritual mediums do, or we can give voice to some larger presence that is trying to work through us as Esther Hicks does. Again, we need to do so from the highest level of intention and love we can imagine if the process is to be beneficial.

The next level of engagement with the world "beyond the veil" is to feel the presence of spiritual beings. These may be people who have passed on or light beings in various forms. Often the first stage is to feel in the body if anything is different in a particular space. Many people are able to feel the holiness of a church or sacred site, and this is similar, though may be more subtle. Many of us have walked into a space and wanted to turn right around and leave because of some sense of, either a past experience we're distressed by, or the presence of energy we don't like – from either the people present or from some other form of being.

As with learning any new skill, we need to learn to honor those sensations and acknowledge them if we're to have more of them, and one way to acknowledge them is to allow our imagination to give them some sort of form – either as a being or as a narrative of an event that has happened, or is happening now, in the space. As we do so, the feeling becomes stronger and we become more sure of ourselves. As we act on that surety, we find that we're more able to sense such things in other circumstances.

To "see" beings that are not in material form requires allowing the inner vision to become more important than the outer eyes. One way to do that is to de-focus the physical eyes and allow the experience of "light shadows" around the edges of one's field of vision. Often we'll see things in our peripheral vision before we can catch them straight on. Sometimes there will be something like a sparkly mist in a space that our unfocused eyes can just barely make out, but that we can learn to allow our awareness to define, explain, and receive information from and about. With practice, those of us who have been trained out of seeing these forms with our normal vision will actually begin to undo that training and discern spirits as clearly as we discern the people we live with.

To prophecy is to receive information from divinity and share it with others. As we develop our ability to allow information to come to us from nonmaterial sources we open the path to prophesy. As we raise our consciousness to a state of love and light and deep appreciation for the good that our creator-source is always offering us, then we can rest assured that whatever messages we receive are for the good of all. As we share those insights, understandings, and any guidance we receive, we can feel a sense of fulfillment and satisfaction, for we are being and doing what we are called and gifted to be an do, for all humanity's sake.

Creating A New World

So where do we go from here?

The world we live in is the result of thousands of years of thought and action by billions of people and sometimes seems like a runaway train that we have no control over. But that's only partly true. As Richard Bach points out in *Illusions*, the beggar of Calcutta, the broker on Wall Street, and Richard flying his plane over fields in Iowa cannot be said to live in the same world. This planet contains as many worlds as groups of people are willing to create.

Yes. We create the world we live in, day by day, thought by thought, action by action. And, like a Google algorithm, this planet always gives us more of what we search for and focus on.

This is not to say we should get all upset about what's around us, because it is, in fact, the product of past thoughts and actions. It is to say, however, that we can start, right here and now, to create the heavenly world we choose to live in. Yes. We can create Heaven on Earth; we just have to let go of the tendency to focus on what isn't heavenly!

To achieve this way of being we need to re-think & reframe our thoughts and actions. We need to:

1. Release what doesn't bring joy
   a. In our life
   b. In our circle
   c. In our world
2. Replace that with a new thought & action in alignment with our current and ongo-ing wellbeing
   a. In our life
   b. In our circle
   c. In our world
3. Be aware of & connect with
   a. Like-minded folks
   b. Related ideas
   c. Opportunities to explore
4. Act from our inner knowing
   a. In our life
   b. In our circle
   c. In our world

And the new thought and action must be really new. We can't use the guidelines of the old way of being to create a new one. We can't assume that anything that worked 5, 10, 100 years ago will ever work again. We *can* draw on experienc-es and understandings from those actions: to the extent that they led to the joyful wellbeing of all those involved then, they may be useful now.

So we need to really think about what is heavenly for us. What does it feel like, look like, taste like, smell like? What past experiences would we joyfully experience more of? What new experiences would feel equally wonderful? Are there particular scenes? Foods? Clothing that feel heavenly? Are there people, or kinds of people, whose presence feels heavenly? Are there ways of being with others? Forms of music? Ways to move your body that feel heavenly? Take some time to just imagine what Heaven on Earth might be, and then write some of that down. Every day for a month if you can. Certainly every few weeks. Imagine your heavenly life on earth and write and draw and sing what it is like.

But here's the important thing: don't think about them feeling "oh, if only..." Write them with gratitude that they're possible! Write them with appreciation for all the ways you've already experienced them! Write them knowing that they are the reality "beyond the veil" that you are now lifting and are ready to experience, for that is, indeed, what this worldwide apocalypse of 2020 is offering us. And no less. Truly.

🕊

About the Author

Ruth L. Miller integrates new understandings of culture and consciousness in a way that "the rest of us" can understand. With degrees in anthropology, environmental studies, cybernetics, and the systems sciences she taught in several colleges and universities while working as a futurist and organizational and community development consultant. Now, having completed a second career as an ordained New Thought minister serving Unity, Science of Mind, and Unitarian churches, she consults, writes, and speaks on the nature of consciousness and spirituality, focused on the future well-being of all humanity. Her website is www.ruthlmillerphd.com

Other Titles by Ruth L Miller from Portal Center Press

Discovering A New Way, possibilities for world peace in the patterns of our past

Empowered Care, mind-body medicine methods *with Robert B. Newman*

Home: choosing humanity's future

Language of Life: solutions to modern crises in an ancient way of speaking, *with Milt Markewitz & Batya Podos*

Making the World Go Away: coping in end times

Mary's Power: embracing the divine feminine as the age of invasion and empire ends

The Power of Creative Thought: Thomas Troward's metaphysics in the modern world

The Science of Mental Healing: lives and teachings of America's New Thought healers

Uncommon Prayer

Unlocking the Power of THE SECRET: 10 keys to transform your thoughts and life

...and check out our many other authors, plus fiction and spiritual explorations, under our imprint: SPIRITBOOKS

www.portalcenterpress.com